HAL LEONARD
BASS METHOD

T0039731

BASS FOR KIDS

A Beginner's Guide with Step-by-Step Instruction for Bass Guitar

BY CHAD JOHNSON

To access audio visit:
www.halleonard.com/mylibrary

Enter Code
6628-8506-7464-9524

Tuning notes are available on Track 71.

Recorded and mixed by Chad Johnson at Tupperware Sounds Studio, NC
Bass: Eric Welch and Brian Pugh
Drums: Adam Moses
Keyboards: Bill Stevens
Guitars: Chad Johnson
Vocals: Chad and Allison Johnson

ISBN 978-1-4234-9848-3

HAL•LEONARD®
CORPORATION
7777 W. BLUEMOUND RD. P.O. BOX 13819 MILWAUKEE, WI 53213

Visit Hal Leonard Online at
www.halleonard.com

SELECTING YOUR BASS

Bass guitars come in three sizes:

And they come in various body shapes:

Full size   3/4 size   1/2 size   "P-bass" style (Precision Bass)   Jazz bass style   Violin style

The P-bass and Jazz bass styles are the most common, and most of the bass guitars you see are based on these shapes. Choose a bass that best fits you.

Too Big   Good Fit

PARTS OF THE BASS

Tuning Pegs

Headstock

Nut

Frets

Neck & Fingerboard

Top "horn"

Position marker

Body

Front (neck) pickup

Back (bridge) pickup

Bottom "horn"

Volume and tone controls

Strap lock

Output jack

HOLDING THE BASS

- Sit up straight and relax your shoulders

- Place your feet flat on the floor or place one foot on a foot stool

- Tilt the neck of the bass slightly upwards

- Raise your thigh and/or adjust your chair or foot stool to prevent the bass from slipping

- Match the body position in the photos below

HAND POSITION

Left Hand

The fingers are numbered 1 through 4 (thumb is not numbered.) Press the string down firmly just behind the fret.

Place your thumb in the middle of the back of the neck and arch your fingers so that your palm doesn't touch the neck.

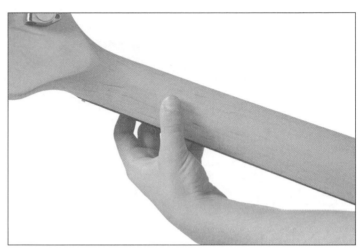

Right Hand

Rest your thumb on the pickup and use your first finger to pluck the string. Push the string slightly inward toward the body of the bass.

When plucking the higher-pitched (thinner) strings, rest your thumb on the lowest pitched (thickest) string to keep it from making noise.

THE 4TH STRING: E

Most basses have four strings, and each one has a note name. They're numbered 1 through 4; 1 is the thinnest, and 4 is the thickest. The 4th string is an E note. We also call this the *lowest* string because it's the lowest in pitch. To play an E note, just pluck the 4th string open.

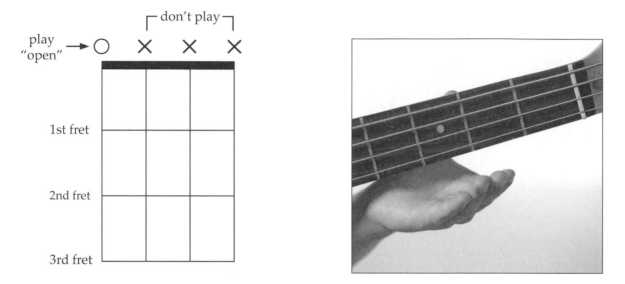

Music is written on a **staff** of five lines and four spaces. Each line or space is assigned a letter name. A **clef** appears at the beginning of every staff. Bass music is written on a bass clef.

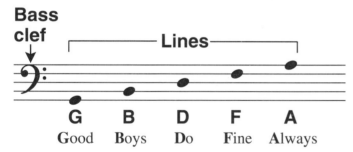

When we write notes above or below the range of the staff, we use **ledger lines**. Our open 4th string is the note E, which is our first ledger line below the staff.

Music has a steady beat, like the ticking of a clock. Count aloud and play each E note slowly and evenly, plucking upward with your first finger.

EASY E JAM   TRACK 1   TRACK 2 SLOW

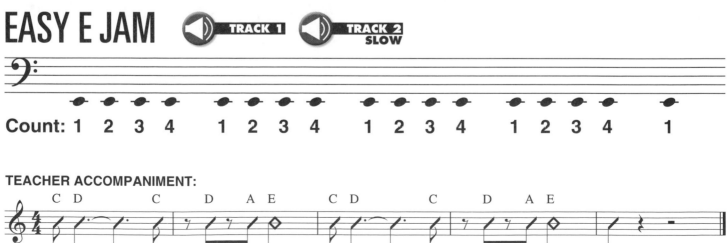

Count: 1 2 3 4   1 2 3 4   1 2 3 4   1 2 3 4   1

TEACHER ACCOMPANIMENT:

THE NOTE F

Use your first finger to press the 4th string at the 1st fret. This is the note F.

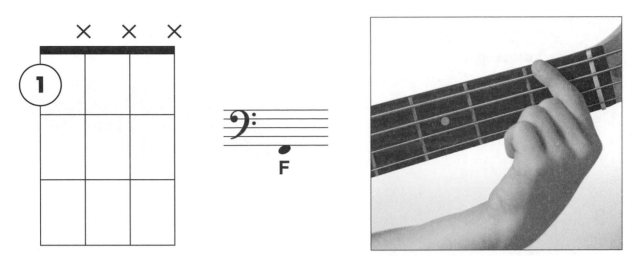

Bar lines divide music into measures. A double bar line means the end.

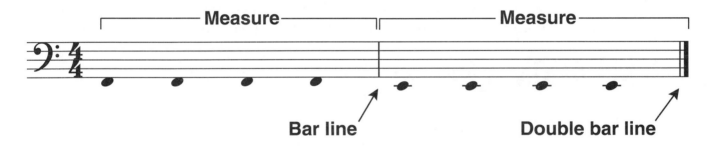

Count aloud as you play this next song. Be sure to keep a steady count!

GREAT WHITE

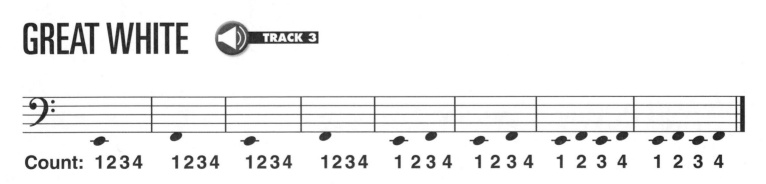

THE NOTE G

The note G is found on the 3rd fret of the 4th string. Use either your third or fourth finger to play it.

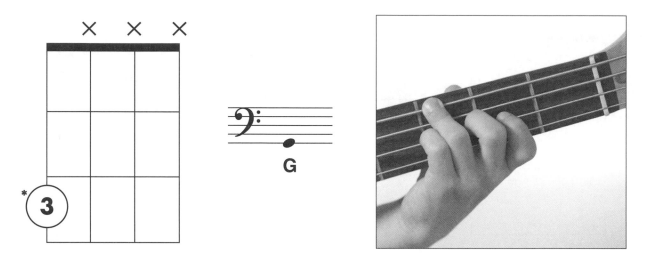

G

*Fourth finger can also be used.

A **time signature** appears at the beginning of a piece of music. It tells how many beats are in each measure and what kind of note is counted as one beat. In 4/4 ("four-four") time, there are four beats in each measure, and a **quarter note** is counted as a beat. It has a solid notehead and a stem (♩).

MY GENERATION   TRACK 4

Time Signature

Count: 1 2 3 4   1 2 3 4   1 2 3 4   1 2 3 4

UP AND DOWN   TRACK 5   TRACK 6 SLOW

Count: 1 2 3 4   1 2 3 4   1 2 3 4

TEACHER ACCOMPANIMENT:

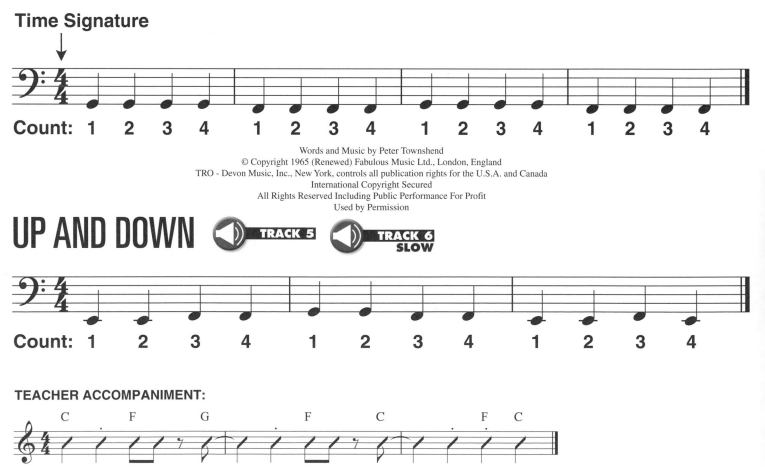

A **half note** (♩) lasts twice as long as a quarter note; it gets two beats.

HALF NOTE ROCK

The F and G notes are all you need to play this classic Fleetwood Mac song.

DREAMS

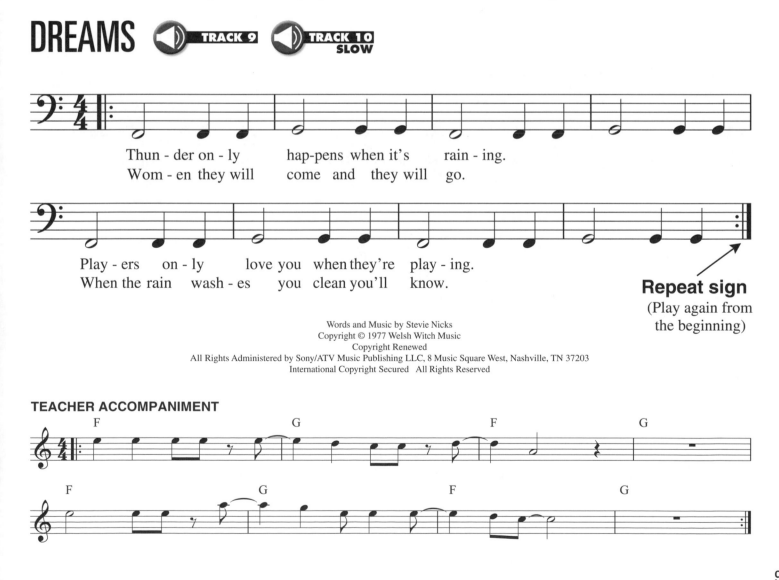

THE 3RD STRING: A

The 3rd string open is the note A. If you're plucking with your fingers, remember you rest your thumb on the 4th string when you pluck the A string.

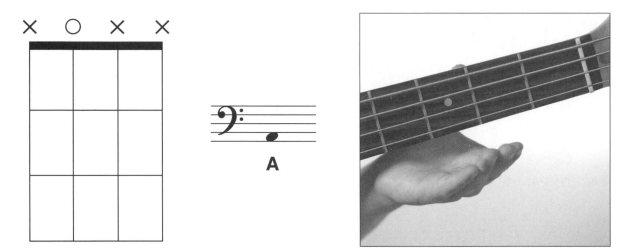

A

You'll see a **chord symbol** in the following song. This tells other instruments (like piano or guitar) what chord to play along with our bass line. When you see chord symbols in music, they're for the teacher (or maybe a friend who plays guitar or piano) to play.

NO SUNSHINE TRACK 11

Teacher plays chord symbols

Am

A **whole note** (o) is twice as long as a half note; it lasts four beats.

BASS STRUT TRACK 12

THE NOTE B

Use your second finger to press the 3rd string at the 2nd fret. This is the note B.

GET UP STAND UP  TRACK 13

Get up, stand up.
Get up, stand up.

Stand up for your right.
Don't give up the fight.

TEACHER ACCOMPANIMENT:

Rests are beats of silence. The **quarter note rest** (𝄽) means to be silent for one beat. To do this, you can lightly touch the strings with your fret hand or plucking finger.

TWO-STRING RIFF TRACK 14

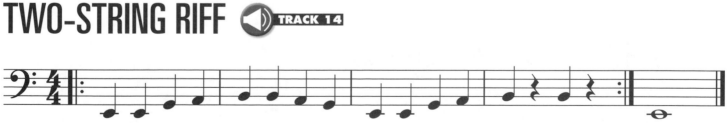

When a dot appears after a note, you extend the note by half its value. A dotted half note ($\scriptstyle\downarrow$.) lasts for three beats.

$$\downarrow + \downarrow = \downarrow.$$

You only need three notes to play this famous song by The Who, and two of them are open strings!

BABA O'RILEY

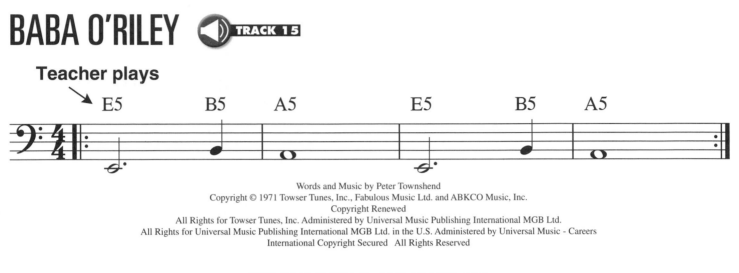

EIGHTH NOTES

An **eighth note** ($\downarrow$) lasts half a beat, or half as long as a quarter note. When several eighth notes appear in a row, they are beamed together.

Eighth notes are counted with the word "and" in between the beats.

DOUBLE TROUBLE

I LOVE ROCK

An **eighth note rest** (𝄾) means to be silent for half a beat.

Be sure to notice the eighth note rests in Jimi Hendrix's classic version of "All Along the Watchtower."

ALL ALONG THE WATCHTOWER

TRACK 20 TRACK 21 SLOW

Intro

Verse

"There must be some kind of way out of here," said the jo - ker to the thief.

There's too much con - fu - sion;

I can't get no re - lief.

(Repeat from beginning of verse)

Additional Lyrics

Businessmen, they drink my wine,
Plowmen they dig my earth.
None of them along the line,
Know what any of it is worth.

Words and Music by Bob Dylan
Copyright © 1968 (Renewed 1996) Dwarf Music
International Copyright Secured   All Rights Reserved

TEACHER ACCOMPANIMENT/MELODY:

Intro

Bm   A   G   A   Bm   A   G   A

Verse

Bm   A   G   A   Bm   A   G   A

Bm   A   G   A   Bm   A   G   A

THE NOTE C

On the 3rd fret of the 3rd string is the note C. Use your third or fourth finger to play it.

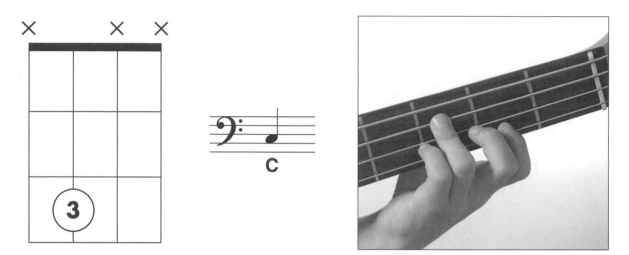

We're playing all whole notes in Eric Clapton's "Wonderful Tonight." Count four full beats for each note so you don't rush them.

WONDERFUL TONIGHT TRACK 22

TEACHER ACCOMPANIMENT/MELODY:

*Play G note second time only

SMELLS LIKE TEEN SPIRIT TRACK 23   TRACK 24 SLOW

NOTE REVIEW

You've learned six notes now: three on the 4th string and three on the 3rd string.

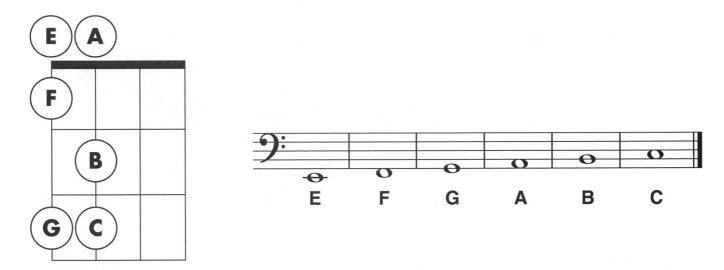

The notes in the following exercises move from string to string. As you play one note, look ahead to the next and get your fingers into position.

THE 2ND STRING: D

The 2nd string open is the note D. Be sure to allow your thumb to rest on the 4th string when you play this string. Also, after you pluck the D string, allow your finger to rest on the 3rd string.

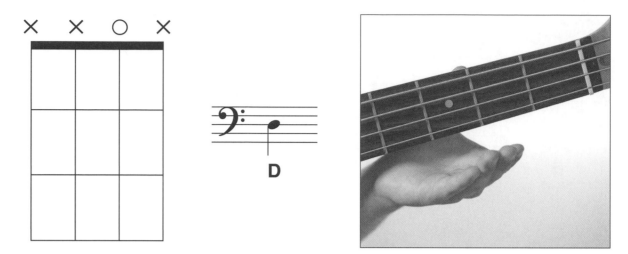

On the Beatles classic, "A Hard Day's Night," you'll get a workout on all three bottom strings.

A HARD DAY'S NIGHT

It's been a hard day's night, and I been work-in' like a dog.

It's been a hard day's night. I should be

sleep-in' like a log. But when I get home to you, I find the

things that you do will make me feel al - right.

TEACHER ACCOMPANIMENT/MELODY:

THE NOTE E (2ND STRING)

The 2nd fret on the 2nd string is the note E. Play this note with your second finger.

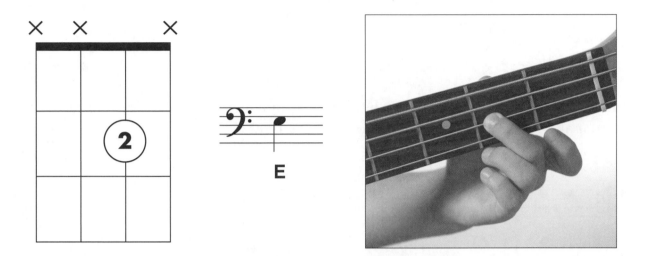

You've already learned another E note. Remember? It's the open 4th string. We say that this E on the 2nd string is an **octave** above the lower one. Play them one after the other to hear how they sound similar. One is just higher than the other.

You'll play both E notes in "Blues Riff."

BLUES RIFF   TRACK 29   TRACK 30 SLOW

A **half note rest** (➖) means to be silent for two beats.

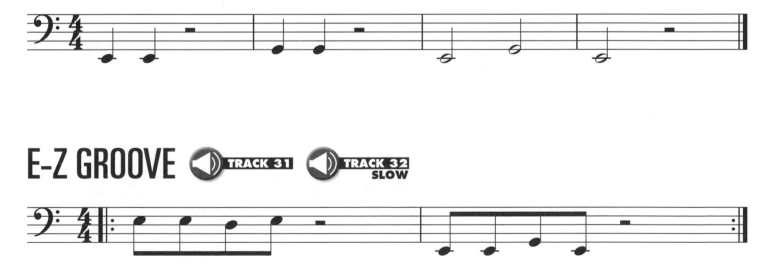

E-Z GROOVE   TRACK 31   TRACK 32 SLOW

TIES

A **tie** (⌣) is a symbol that connects two notes and tells you to hold the first note through the end of the second note.

𝅗𝅥 ⌣ 𝅗𝅥 = 𝅗𝅥   𝅗𝅥 ⌣ 𝅗𝅥 = 𝅝   𝅗𝅥 ⌣ 𝅗𝅥 = 𝅗𝅥.

You can tie any two notes of the same pitch together. Count aloud during this exercise and listen to the audio to make sure you're holding the notes for the right length.

TRACK 33

Count: 1 2 (3 4)   1 (2 3) 4   1 2 & (3) 4   1 2 (3) & 4

WILD THING   TRACK 34   TRACK 35 SLOW

Intro

A   D   E   **Chorus**
                                             A   D

Wild   thing,

E   D   A   D   E   D

you   make my heart   sing.   You make ev-

A   D   E   D

'ry - thing   groov - y

A   D   E   A

Wild   thing.

Words and Music by Chip Taylor
© 1965 (Renewed 1993) EMI BLACKWOOD MUSIC INC.
All Rights Reserved International Copyright Secured Used by Permission

THE RAKE

When we move quickly from a higher pitched string to a lower pitched one, we use a **rake**. This means we drag the same finger across to pluck both strings in one smooth motion.

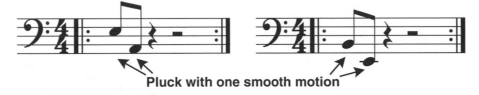

The next song begins with a **pickup note**. Count the missing beats out loud before you start.

Words and Music by William "Smokey" Robinson and Ronald White

TEACHER ACCOMPANIMENT/MELODY:

THE NOTE F (2ND STRING)

The 3rd fret on the 2nd string is the note F. Use either your 3rd or 4th finger to play it.

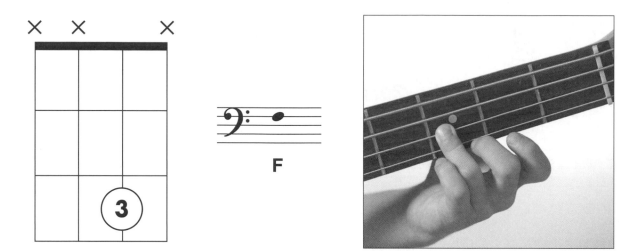

The other F we know is an octave below on the 1st fret of the 4th string. Play the two F notes to hear how they sound similar, and then play the riff below in "Grapevine."

GRAPEVINE

Just as we had dotted half notes, we can also have a **dotted quarter note**. This note lasts for one and a half beats, or the same as a quarter note and an eighth note tied together. This is a very popular rhythm in bass lines.

STROLLIN' DOWN THE LANE

TEACHER ACCOMPANIMENT:

Now let's learn a song that uses almost all of the notes we've learned so far. We're playing nothing but half notes and whole notes here.

IMAGINE

ROOT—5TH SHAPE

A very common approach in bass playing is called the "root–5th." The **root** is simply the note that a chord is named after; it's what we bass players normally play. The **5th** is five note names higher than the root. If we count up five from A, we find that E is the 5th of A.

A	B	C	D	E
1	2	3	4	5

On the bass, 5ths are very easy to find. The 5th is always up a string and up two frets.

You can move anywhere on the bass, and this shape will always be a root and a 5th.

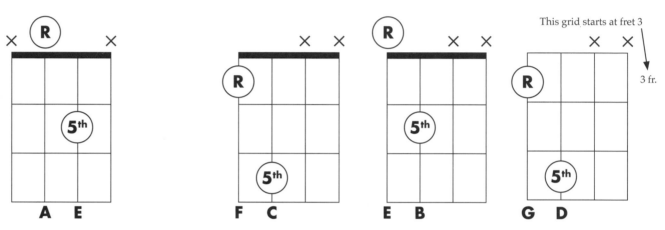

The last grid above started at fret 3 and used the 3rd and 5th frets. This also demonstrates that we can play the same note on different places on the bass. In fact, most notes can be played at several spots on the bass. The D note on the 5th fret of the 3rd string is the same exact note as the open 2nd string. Play them one after the other to hear this.

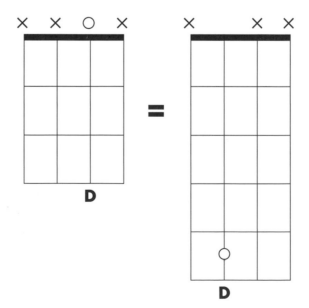

Bass players sometimes alternate between the root and 5th to create a little more excitement in the bass line.

ROOT—5TH ROCK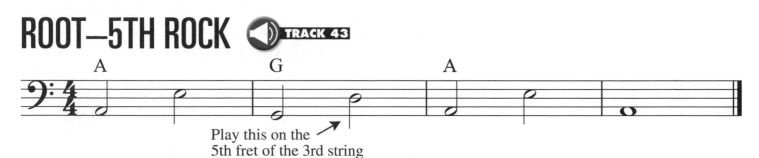

We use the root-5th approach to play the Beatles classic, "Love Me Do." In this song, we use two different root-5th shapes: G-D and C-G. They both use the 3rd and 5th frets.

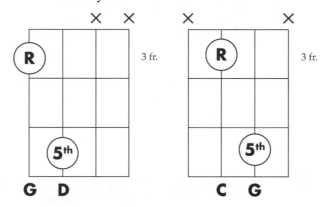

The tempo (speed of the music) is a little quicker here, but we're not playing very many notes.

LOVE ME DO

Love, love me do. You know I love you. I'll

always be true. So please

love me do. Oh, love me do.

TEACHER ACCOMPANIMENT/MELODY:

ALTERNATE PLUCKING

When we play a lot of eighth notes in a row, it's best to **alternate plucking** with the 1st and 2nd fingers. This allows us to play faster and still be relaxed. You can try starting with your 1st or 2nd finger.

In this next jam, you may notice that measure 2 sounds messy. To fix this, lightly touch the open D string with a fret-hand finger after you play it, so that it doesn't keep ringing when you go back to the open A string. This is called **muting**, and it helps to keep our bass lines clean.

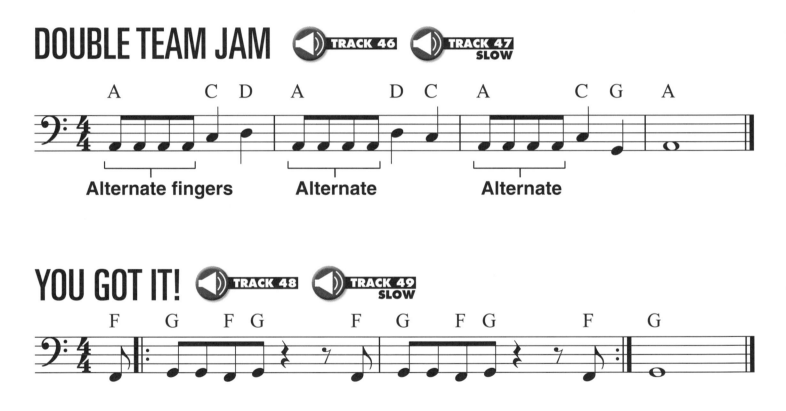

Here you're going to get practice alternating plucking fingers on different strings. If you need to, start slowly and build up to the speed on the track.

24

You're now ready to tackle this classic bass line from U2's "With or Without You." It's all eighth notes on this one!

WITH OR WITHOUT YOU

See the stone   set in your eyes,   see the thorn   twist in your side.

I wait   for you.

Sleight of hand   and twist of fate   on a   bed of nails   she   makes me wait.

And I wait   without you,   with or without you,

with or without you.

Words by Bono and The Edge
Music by U2
Copyright © 1987 UNIVERSAL MUSIC PUBLISHING INTERNATIONAL B.V.
All Rights in the U.S. and Canada Controlled and Administered by UNIVERSAL - POLYGRAM INTERNATIONAL PUBLISHING, INC.
All Rights Reserved   Used by Permission

TEACHER ACCOMPANIMENT/MELODY:

etc.

THE FIRST STRING: G AND A NOTES

The open 1st string is the note G. The A note is located at the 2nd fret.

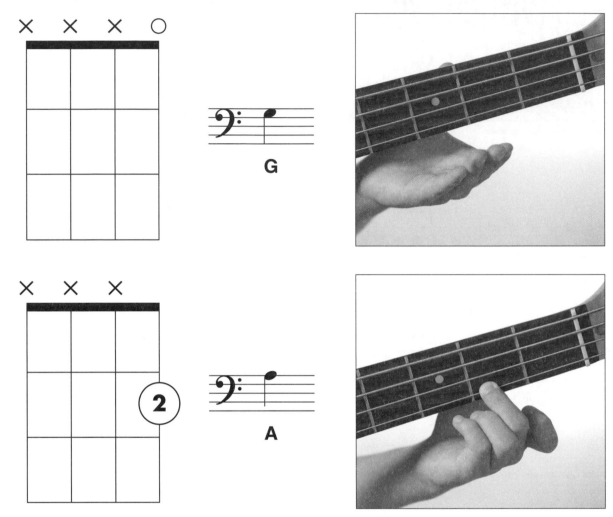

G

A

DRIVIN' RIFF

A7

ROCKIN' THE OCTAVES

A   G   E   A   E

OCTAVE SHAPE

Another handy visual aid is the **octave shape**. Just like the root-5th shape, it's the same on the bass no matter where you play it. An octave on the bass is always up two strings and two frets.

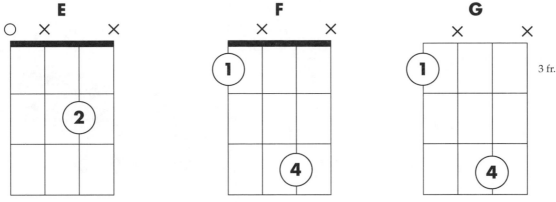

When you play an octave shape with two fretted notes (no open strings), it's best to use your 1st finger for the low string and your 4th finger (pinky) for the high string. This is because the frets on the bass are far apart, and it would be hard to reach the top note with your 3rd finger. When you do use your pinky, you can lay your 3rd finger behind it to help push the string down.

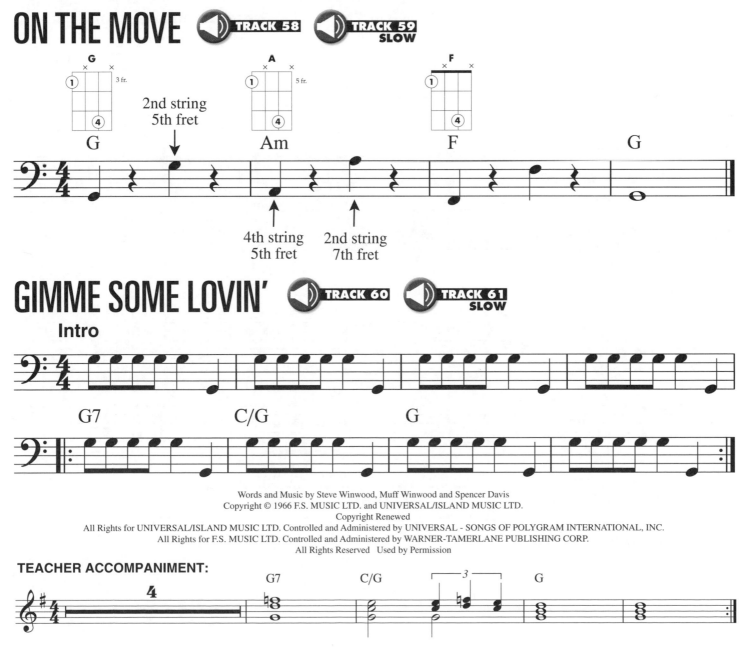

THE NOTE F♯

Sharp (♯) and **flat** (♭) notes are called **accidentals**. A sharp note is one fret higher than a normal note, and a flat note is one fret lower. The note F♯ is found at the 2nd fret of the 4th string—one fret higher than the note F.

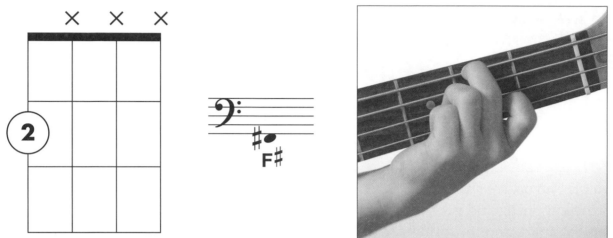

When we want to return a note back to normal (not sharp or flat), we use a **natural** sign (♮). We'll see this in our next song, so watch out for it!

CHICAGO GROOVE TRACK 62 TRACK 63 SLOW

Natural sign

CRAZY TRAIN TRACK 64 TRACK 65 SLOW

Intro

Play 3 times

D5   E   A

Words and Music by Ozzy Osbourne, Randy Rhoads and Bob Daisley
Copyright © 1981 Blizzard Music Limited, 12 Thayer Street, London, W1M 5LD, England
International Copyright Secured   All Rights Reserved

TEACHER ACCOMPANIMENT:

Play 3 times

D5   E   A

MAJOR SCALE

A scale is a collection of notes used to make melodies, chords, and bass lines. A **major scale** is a happy-sounding scale. Here's a G major scale shape based off the G note on the 4th string.

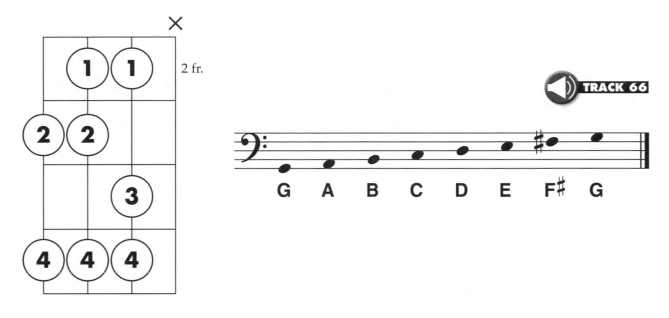

You can move this shape up or down the neck to play other major scales.

1–3–5 SHAPE

If you take the 1st, 3rd, and 5th notes of the G major scale we just played, you have a 1–3–5 shape.

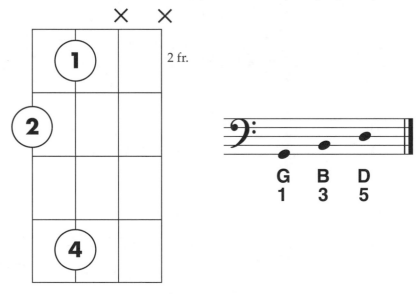

Like the root-5th shape, many bass lines are built using this type of shape too. And you can also move this shape around to play the 1–3–5 pattern from different root notes.

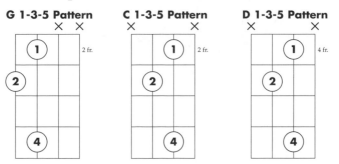

G 1-3-5 Pattern   C 1-3-5 Pattern   D 1-3-5 Pattern

29

Let's use this 1–3–5 shape in a famous Bob Marley song.

STIR IT UP

Stir it up,   little darling.   Stir it up.

TEACHER ACCOMPANIMENT/MELODY:

In this final song, you're going to use all the notes you've learned so far!

EVERY BREATH YOU TAKE

Intro

Verse

Every breath you

take,   every move you make,   every bond you break,

every step you take,   I'll be watching you.   Oh   can't you

CERTIFICATE OF ACHIEVEMENT

Congratulations to

_____

(YOUR NAME)

_____

(DATE)

You have completed

BASS FOR KIDS

_____

(TEACHER SIGNATURE)

You are now ready for

HAL LEONARD BASS METHOD BOOK 1